Department of the Environment
Welsh Office

PLANNING POLICY GUIDANCE:

GENERAL POLICY AND PRINCIPLES

Introduction

1.   This Planning Policy Guidance Note is a revision of PPG1, first published in January 1988, which it supersedes. The guidance in the earlier version has been reviewed and amended to reflect changes introduced by the Planning and Compensation Act 1991 and developments in policy stemming, in particular, from the White Paper "This Common Inheritance", published in September 1990. It sets out the general principles under which the planning system is to operate and incorporates advice on some specific issues not covered elsewhere in PPGs.

2.   The town and country planning system is designed to regulate the development and use of land in the public interest. The system has served the country well. It is an important instrument for protecting and enhancing the environment in town and country, preserving the built and natural heritage, conserving the rural landscape and maintaining Green Belts.

3.   The Government has made clear its intention to work towards ensuring that development and growth are sustainable. It will continue to develop policies consistent with the concept of sustainable development. The planning system, and the preparation of development plans in particular, can contribute to the objectives of ensuring that development and growth are sustainable. The sum total of decisions in the planning field, as elsewhere, should not deny future generations the best of today's environment.

4.   The planning system has a positive role to play in guiding appropriate development to the right place, as well as preventing development which is not acceptable. It must make adequate provision for development (for example, the new houses and workplaces the nation needs, and associated services such as roads and schools), and at the same time take account of the need to protect the natural and built environment. It must also take account of international obligations. In this way, properly used, the planning system can secure economy, efficiency and amenity in the use of land.

5.   The planning system should be efficient, effective and simple in conception and operation. It fails in its function whenever it prevents, inhibits or delays development which should reasonably have been permitted. It should operate on the basis that applications for development should be allowed, having regard to the development plan and all material considerations, unless the proposed development would cause demonstrable harm to interests of acknowledged importance. The approach that decision makers should take to the consideration of planning applications is set out in paragraphs 25-31 below.

6.   It is not the function of the planning system to interfere with or inhibit competition between users and investors in land, or to regulate the overall provision and character of space for particular uses for other than land-use planning reasons. Where development is acceptable, it is a matter for landowners, developers and/or tenants as to whether or not to proceed with it.

> ### Speed of Operation
> Unnecessary delays in the planning system can result in extra costs, wasted capital, delayed production, reduced employment opportunities, and lost income and productivity. The Government and local planning authorities therefore have a responsibility to ensure that delays in preparing development plans, and in determining planning applications and appeals are minimised. Local planning authorities should aim to decide 80% of applications within eight weeks.
>
> The target handling times for appeal cases decided by Inspectors are being reviewed in preparation for the Planning Inspectorate's transition to a 'Next Steps' Executive Agency on 1 April 1992. The targets, which will be published, will be compatible with the standards of efficiency and effectiveness that the Government wishes to see reflected elsewhere in the planning system. Where the Secretaries of State take the decision on appeals, they will aim to decide 80% of cases within eight weeks of receiving the Inspector's report.

Legislation

7.   The primary legislation is now contained in three consolidating Acts of Parliament:

the Town and Country Planning Act 1990 (referred to in this guidance as "the 1990 Act");

the Planning (Listed Buildings and Conservation Areas) Act 1990; and

the Planning (Hazardous Substances) Act 1990 (when brought into force).

Each of these Acts has been amended by the Planning and Compensation Act 1991 (referred to in this guidance as "the 1991 Act").

8.   The main instruments of subordinate legislation are: the Town and Country Planning General Development Order 1988 (the GDO) and the Town and Country Planning (Use Classes) Order 1987 (the UCO), both of which have been amended; and the Town and Country Planning (Development Plan) Regulations 1991.

Planning Permission

9.   Planning permission is required for any development of land. "Development" is defined in section 55 of the 1990 Act as "the carrying out of building, engineering, mining or other operations in, on, over or under land, or the making of any material change in the use of any buildings or other land". The definition of building operations will be amended (when section 13 of the 1991 Act is brought into force) to include the demolition of buildings. A direction by the Secretaries of State and amendments to the GDO will have the effect that most types of demolition will either not involve development or will be permitted development.

10.   Section 55 also provides that certain works and uses do not constitute development under the Act. These include:

works of maintenance, improvement or alteration which affect only the interior of a building or which do not materially affect its external appearance;

the use of buildings or land within the curtilage of a dwellinghouse for any purpose incidental to the enjoyment of the dwellinghouse as such;

the use of land for the purpose of agriculture or forestry; and

change of use of land or buildings from one use to another within the same class of the UCO.

11.   Moreover, the GDO, as amended, gives a general permission for certain defined classes of development or use of land, mainly of a minor character. The most commonly used class permits a wide range of small extensions or alterations to dwellinghouses. Schemes for Enterprise Zones and Simplified Planning Zones (see PPG5) also confer planning permission for developments of types defined in the scheme concerned.

12.   The general permission which the GDO grants for a particular development or class of development may be withdrawn in a particular area by a direction made by the local authority or by the Secretaries of State under Article 4 of the GDO. Where this is done, specific permission for the development in question must be sought, although refusal of permission in these circumstances or the granting of permission subject to conditions (other than those imposed by the GDO) entitles those with an interest in the land to claim compensation from the local planning authority under sections 107 and 108 of the 1990 Act, for any financial loss and/or depreciation in the value of the land.

13.   Currently over 500,000 planning applications are received by English local authorities annually, and nearly 40,000 by those in Wales. About 80% are granted. The Secretaries of State may require applications to be referred to them for decision, but this call-in power has in recent years only been exercised in around 130 cases each year in England, and in about 10 in Wales. The policy of the Secretaries of State is to be very selective about calling in planning applications, and such action is generally taken only if planning issues of more than local importance are involved. Examples are applications which could have wide effects beyond their immediate area, or give rise to substantial controversy nationally or regionally, or conflict with national policy on important matters, or where national security or the interests of foreign governments are involved.

14.   Under section 78 of the 1990 Act, an applicant may appeal to the respective Secretary of State against a local planning authority's decision to refuse planning permission or to grant it subject to conditions, or against the authority's failure to notify its decision within 8 weeks or within a longer period that may have been agreed between the applicant and the authority. The Department of the Environment and the Welsh Office currently receive some 25,000 planning appeals a year, of which about one-third are allowed. The overwhelming majority (98%) of the planning permissions granted in England and Wales each year result from decisions by local planning authorities; only 2% from decisions by the Secretaries of State or Planning Inspectors following call-in or on appeal.

15.   Planning authorities have an extensive and flexible range of discretionary enforcement powers with which to deal with breaches of planning control. The 1991 Act introduces a new planning contravention notice, a breach of condition notice and a provision for obtaining an injunction to restrain a breach of planning control, in addition to improving and strengthening the present powers to issue an enforcement notice and serve a stop notice. These new provisions will make the planning powers more effective. Guidance on their use is given in PPG18 and DOE Circular 21/91 (WO 76/91).

16.   In deciding whether to grant planning permission, decision-makers must refer to the provisions of the development plan (see paragraphs 25-31 below) and to all other material considerations. In every case where a proposal for develop-

ment is not acceptable, the local planning authority must state clearly and precisely the full reasons for refusing planning permission. Similarly, where the Secretaries of State refuse a planning application on appeal, or following a call-in, they must give their reasons for that decision. Local planning authorities should also be prepared on request to explain to a statutory consultee, where they decide to approve an application against the advice of that consultee, the reasons for their approval.

Development Plans

17. Full guidance on the preparation of development plans is given in PPG12, and for Wales in PPG 12 (Wales). Development plans are prepared following a statutory process of public consultation and debate. Such plans, which should be consistent with national and regional planning policy, provide the primary means of reconciling conflicts between the need for development, including the provision of infrastructure, and the need to protect the built and natural environment. Although their provisions are not prescriptive, they are intended to provide a firm basis for rational and consistent decisions on planning applications and appeals. Statutorily approved and adopted plans provide all concerned with development in a locality – residents and amenity bodies, developers and other business interests, and those responsible for providing infrastructure – with a measure of certainty about what types of development will and will not be permitted.

18. A number of different plans may together comprise the development plan – depending on the subject and the area where development is proposed. These plans comprise:

(i) *structure plans*, setting out strategic policies in non-metropolitan areas;

(ii) *local plans, waste local plans* and *minerals local plans*, all of which set out detailed development policies for non-metropolitan areas;

(iii) *unitary development plans* in which planning authorities in Greater London and metropolitan areas combine the functions of (i) and (ii);

and for a transitional period:

(iv) *old-style development plans* approved under legislation up to and including the Town and Country Planning Act 1962 and not yet replaced by local plan provisions; and

(v) any local plan saved under Schedule 4 to the 1991 Act.

Structure plans are already in place for all areas in England and Wales. Unitary development plans are in preparation for all metropolitan areas and Greater London. The 1991 Act makes mandatory the preparation of district-wide and National Park-wide local plans, and of county-wide and National Park-wide minerals and waste local plans. The Secretaries of State expect coverage of area-wide local plans to be substantially complete by the end of 1996.

19. The Secretaries of State are statutory consultees in the preparation of development plans, and have powers of intervention – they can object to a draft plan on deposit, or direct that a draft plan should be modified, or ultimately they can call in all or part of a draft plan for their own determination.

Statements of the Government's Planning Policies

20. The Courts have held that the Government's statements of planning policy are material considerations which must be taken into account, where relevant, in decisions on planning applications. Such policy statements may be found in White Papers; Planning Policy Guidance Notes (PPGs); Minerals Planning Guidance Notes (MPGs); Regional Planning Guidance Notes (RPGs) [England only]; Development Control Policy Notes (DCPNs); Departmental Circulars; and Ministerial statements. PPGs, MPGs and RPGs are now the principal source of policy guidance on planning matters; DCPNs are being progressively withdrawn, and planning Circulars will tend to focus on legislative and procedural matters.

21. The Department's policy statements cannot make irrelevant any matter which is a material consideration in a particular case. But where such statements indicate the weight that should be given to relevant considerations, decision-makers must have proper regard to them. If decision-makers elect not to follow relevant statements of the Government's planning policy they must give clear and convincing reasons (*E C Gransden and Co Ltd v. SSE and Gillingham BC 1985*).

22. Emerging policies, in the form of draft Departmental Circulars and policy guidance, are capable of being regarded as material considerations, depending on the context. It may not be appropriate to disregard such drafts completely, since their very existence may indicate that a relevant policy is under review; and the circumstances which have led to that review may need to be taken into account.

Other Material Considerations

23. "In principle ... any consideration which relates to the use and development of land is capable of being a planning consideration. Whether a particular consideration falling within that broad class is material in any given case will depend on the circumstances" (*Stringer v. MHLG 1971*). Material considerations must be genuine planning considerations, ie they must be related to the purpose of planning legislation, which is to regulate the development and use of land in the public interest. The considerations must also fairly and reasonably relate to the application concerned

(*R v. Westminster CC ex parte Monahan 1989*). Much will depend on the nature of the application under consideration, the relevant policies in the development plan and the surrounding circumstances.

24. The Courts are the arbiters of what constitutes a material consideration. Over the years the scope of what can be regarded as material has been clarified by judicial authority. All the fundamental factors involved in land-use planning are included, such as the number, size, layout, siting, design and external appearance of buildings and the proposed means of access, together with landscaping, impact on the neighbourhood and the availability of infrastructure.

Determining planning applications and appeals

25. The approach that decision-makers should take to the consideration of planning applications is set out in sections 70(2) and 54A of the 1990 Act (the latter inserted by section 26 of the 1991 Act). Section 70(2) requires the decision-maker to have regard to the development plan, so far as it is material to the application, and to any other material considerations. Where the development plan is material to the development proposal, and must therefore be taken into account, section 54A requires the application or appeal to be determined in accordance with the plan, unless material considerations indicate otherwise. In effect, this introduces a presumption in favour of development proposals which are in accordance with the development plan. An applicant who proposes a development which is clearly in conflict with the development plan would need to produce convincing reasons to demonstrate why the plan should not prevail. (The plan to which sections 70(2) and 54A apply is the approved or adopted development plan for the area, and not any draft plan which may exist – but see paragraph 32 below).

26. Those deciding planning applications or appeals should therefore look to see whether the development plan contains policies or proposals which are relevant to the particular development proposal. Such material policies and proposals may either give support to a development proposal in a particular location or indicate that it is not appropriate. If the development plan does contain material policies or proposals and there are no other material considerations, the application or appeal should be determined in accordance with the development plan.

27. Where there are other material considerations, the development plan should be taken as a starting point, and the other material considerations should be weighed in reaching a decision. One such consideration will be whether the development plan policies are up-to-date and apply to current circumstances, or whether they have been overtaken by events (the age of the plan is not in itself material). For example, policies and proposals in the plan may have been superseded by more recent planning guidance issued by the Government, or developments since the plan became operative may have rendered certain policies or proposals in the plan incapable of implementation or out of date.

28. In those cases where the development plan is not relevant, for example because the plan does not contain a policy relating to a particular development proposal, or there are material policies in the plan which pull in opposite directions so that the plan does not provide a clear guide for a particular proposal, the planning application or appeal should be determined on its merits in the light of all the material considerations.

29. Since the commencement of section 54A, the Secretaries of State have been examining development plans carefully to identify whether there appear to be conflicts with national or regional policy guidance. They will continue to do so and will normally draw the attention of local authorities to those conflicts which do not appear to be justified by local circumstances. If necessary they will make a formal intervention (see paragraph 19 above); if no such intervention is made, local authorities may take it that the Secretaries of State are content with the plan at the time of adoption and will attach commensurate weight to it in decisions they make on appeals or called-in applications.

30. Local planning authorities or the Secretaries of State may find it appropriate, on occasion, to permit a development proposal which departs from the development plan because the particular contribution of that proposal to some local or national need or objective is so significant that it outweighs what the plan has to say about it. Such a consideration might be, for example, compelling argument by the applicant or appellant that a particular proposal should be allowed to proceed because of the contribution it will make to fulfilling an international commitment, or to some other particular objective which the plan did not foresee or address. Certain departures (see the Town and Country Planning Development Plans Directions 1992 for England and Wales) must be notified to the Secretary of State concerned so that he can decide whether to call in the application for his own decision.

31. There will be occasions when a planning authority can show that the determination of a planning application for a proposed development is in accordance with an operative plan which is up-to-date and consistent with national and regional policies, and has substantiated this in its reasons for refusal of permission and in its written statement on an appeal. In such circumstances, the applicant will risk an award of the authority's costs against him if he pursues the appeal to a hearing or an inquiry but is unable to produce substantial evidence to support the contention that there are material considerations which

would justify an exception to the policies in the plan. An applicant who presses to appeal a matter which is dealt with in a well-advanced draft development plan, where the planning authority has refused the application on grounds of "prematurity" (see paragraphs 32-34 below), also risks having costs awarded against him if his action in pressing the appeal in advance of the plan's adoption is found to be unreasonable.

Prematurity

32. The weight to be attached to emerging development plans which are going through the statutory procedures towards adoption, depends upon the stage of preparation – the weight will increase as successive stages are reached – and upon the degree of any conflict with the existing plans. If no objections have been lodged to relevant policies in a deposited plan, then considerable weight may be attached to those policies because of the strong possibility that they will be adopted and replace those in the existing plan.

33. Questions of prematurity may arise where a development plan is in preparation or under review, and proposals have been issued for consultation, but the plan has not yet been adopted or approved. In these circumstances it may be justifiable to refuse planning permission on grounds of prematurity in respect of development proposals which are individually so substantial, or likely to be so significant cumulatively, as to predetermine decisions about scale, location or phasing of new development which ought properly to be taken in the development plan context. However, whenever possible, planning applications should continue to be considered in the light of current policies. Where planning permission is refused on grounds of prematurity, at a time when the development plan is being prepared or reviewed, the planning authority will need to indicate clearly how the grant of permission for the development concerned would prejudice the outcome of the development plan process; rejection on grounds of prematurity would not normally be justified in cases where the effect on the plan would be marginal.

34. Where there is a phasing policy in the development plan [see paragraphs 5.38-5.42 of PPG12, and 5.36-5.40 of PPG12 (Wales)] there may be circumstances in which it is necessary to refuse planning permission on grounds of prematurity if the policy is to have effect.

Other Legislation

35. Decisions on individual applications should be based on planning grounds only, and must be reasonable. Planning legislation should not normally be used to secure objectives achievable under other legislation. This principle of non-duplication should be maintained even though the powers and duties resulting from the other legislation may also be the concern of local authorities. But even where consent is needed under other legislation, the planning system may have an important part to play, for example in deciding whether the development is appropriate for the particular location. The grant of planning permission does not remove the need to obtain any other consents that may be necessary, nor does it imply that such consents will necessarily be forthcoming.

36. For example, the Building Regulations impose requirements on how most non-domestic buildings should be designed and constructed to secure specific objectives relating to health and safety, access for disabled people and energy conservation. It would not be appropriate to use planning legislation to impose *separate* requirements in these areas, although development plan policies can seek to ensure that consideration is given to the provision of adequate access for disabled people in the preparation of site layouts and in the relationship between buildings and their carparking areas and other public access points. Such factors can also be taken into account in determining planning applications. However, detailed attention to the precise standard of provision – for example, the specifications for steps, ramps and doors – should not be dealt with under planning legislation. Similarly, a planning application for, say, an amusement centre should be considered on its land-use planning merits and not on the basis of issues which are immaterial to those considerations, such as moral grounds or because it is considered that the demand for such facilities is already met in the area. Licences for amusement centres offering prizes must be obtained under the Gaming Acts. The grant of such licences is at the discretion of local authorities who may take into account, among other things, the fact that the demand for such facilities is already adequately met in a particular area.

37. Provided a consideration is material in planning terms, however, it must be taken into account in dealing with a planning application notwithstanding that other machinery may exist for its regulation. For example, planning permission may be refused on the ground that the land concerned forms part of a proposed road widening scheme, even though an alternative procedure is specified in the Highways Act (*Westminster Bank Ltd v. MHLG 1971*).

Personal Circumstances

38. Unless otherwise specified, a planning permission runs with the land and it is seldom desirable to provide for any other arrangement. Exceptionally, however, the personal circumstances of an occupier, personal hardship, or the difficulties of businesses which are of value to the character of the local community, may be material to the consideration of a planning application. In such circumstances, a permission may be made subject to a condition that it is personal to the applicant (see paragraph 73 of Annex to DOE and WO Circular 1/85). Such arguments will seldom outweigh the more general planning considerations. If the proposed development entails works

of a permanent nature they will remain long after the personal circumstances of the applicant have ceased to be material.

Third Party Interests

39. The planning system does not exist to protect the private interests of one person against the activities of another, although private interests may coincide with the public interest in some cases. In fact "the public interest ... may require that the interests of individual occupiers should be considered. The protection of individual interests is one aspect, and an important one, of the public interest as a whole" (*Stringer v. MHLG 1971*).

40. It is often difficult to distinguish between public and private interests, but this may be necessary on occasion. The basic question is not whether owners and occupiers of neighbouring properties would experience financial or other loss from a particular development, but whether the proposal would unacceptably affect amenities and the existing use of land and buildings which ought to be protected in the public interest. Good neighbourliness and fairness are among the yardsticks against which development proposals can be measured, for example it might be material to consider the question of 'overlooking' or loss of privacy experienced by a particular resident. Furthermore, planning permission may be refused where a proposed development would have an adverse effect on a nearby existing development provided there is a planning purpose or other special consideration involved, eg the siting of a ready-mixed concrete plant adjacent to a high precision plant requiring especially clean air (*RMC Management Services Ltd v. SSE 1972*).

41. The Government recognises the importance of public awareness of, and participation in, the development control process. It is committed to requiring publicity for all planning applications to augment the legislation which already provides for registers of all planning applications to be available for public inspection. Local inquiries and hearings into planning appeals and called-in applications are held in public and members of the public have an opportunity to express views on the proposed development. Similarly, when appeals are decided on the basis of written representations, the planning authorities notify those likely to be affected by the development proposal and it is open to them to express their views in writing.

42. In general, the elected members of the local planning authority represent the interests of the community in planning matters. But when determining planning applications they must take into account any relevant views on planning matters expressed by neighbouring occupiers, local residents and any other third parties. For example, opponents of a development proposal may highlight factors, such as traffic problems or the scale of a proposed development in relation to its surroundings, which are land-use planning issues and thus comprise material considerations; these must be taken into account, along with all other material considerations, in deciding the case. Nevertheless, local opposition to a proposal is not in itself a ground for refusing planning permission, unless that opposition is founded upon valid planning reasons which can be substantiated. While the substance of local opposition must be considered, the duty is to decide each case on its planning merits.

Environmental Assessment

43. Environmental assessment (EA) is a process by which information about the likely environmental effects of certain major projects is collected, assessed and taken into account by the local planning authority in deciding whether planning permission should be granted. The Town and Country Planning (Assessment of Environmental Effects) Regulations 1988, which implement a European Community Directive, set out two lists of projects. For those in Schedule 1 (such as crude oil refineries, major aerodromes and the disposal of radioactive or other toxic waste), EA is required to be carried out in every case. For the wider list in Schedule 2 (including the chemical, food, textile and rubber industries, minerals extraction and the disposal of non-toxic waste), EA is required if the particular development proposed is judged likely to have significant effects on the environment by virtue of factors such as its nature, size or location.

44. Where EA is required, the applicant must prepare and submit an environmental statement with the planning application. An applicant may submit an environmental statement voluntarily, but otherwise it will fall to the local planning authority to decide whether EA is necessary. An applicant who is dissatisfied with the authority's request for EA may seek a direction from the relevant Secretary of State as to whether EA is required.

45. Further information on these requirements is given in DOE Circular 15/88 (WO 23/88) and in the Department's booklet "Environmental Assessment – A Guide to the Procedures" (HMSO, November 1989).

Planning Conditions

46. The ability of local planning authorities and the Secretaries of State to impose conditions on a planning permission can enable many development proposals to proceed where it would otherwise be necessary to refuse planning permission. The sensitive use of conditions can improve the quality of development control and enhance public confidence in the planning system. To achieve these ends, conditions should be used in a way which is clearly seen to be fair, reasonable and practicable. Conditions should only be imposed where they are:

  * necessary
  * relevant to planning
  * relevant to the development to be permitted
  * enforceable
  * precise
  * reasonable in all other respects.

47. In considering whether a particular condition is necessary, one key test is whether planning

permission would have to be refused if the condition were not imposed. If not, then such a condition needs special and precise justification. The same criteria and test should be applied in deciding whether to dispense with an extant condition. More detailed advice about planning conditions is given in DOE Circular 1/85 (WO 1/85), and for mineral developments in MPGs 2 and 7.

Planning Obligations

48.   Guidance on the operation of section 106 of the 1990 Act, as substituted by section 12 of the 1991 Act, and on the use of planning obligations, is given in DOE Circular 16/91 (WO 53/91).

Listed Building Control

49.   The Planning (Listed Buildings and Conservation Areas) Act 1990 sets out an additional system of control for listed buildings and conservation areas. Under these provisions listed building consent is needed for any works to demolish a listed building, or to alter or extend it in any manner which would affect its character as a building of special architectural or historic interest. Separate controls also apply to the demolition of most unlisted buildings in conservation areas. These controls are additional to any planning permission or other consents which may be necessary. Advice on the operation of listed building and conservation area controls in England and Wales is given respectively in DOE Circular 8/87 and WO Circular 61/81.

Design Considerations

50.   Guidance on design considerations is given in Annex A.

Crime Prevention

51.   Crime prevention is one of the social considerations to which, in accordance with the Town and Country (Development Plan) Regulations 1991, regard must be given in development plans. Local plans may establish standards for the design and layout of new development which can make crime more difficult to commit and/or increase the risk of detection for potential offenders. Local authorities may also wish to consult Police Architectural Liaison Officers (ALOs) on planning applications for those developments where there is potential to eliminate or reduce criminal activity through the adoption of appropriate measures at the design stage. Because there are very few ALOs they should be consulted mainly on applications which involve a large number of people or properties, for example new housing estates, industrial estates, shopping centres, leisure complexes and car parks. More detailed advice on crime prevention will be contained in a future Circular.

Hazardous Substances

52.   The controls in the Planning (Hazardous Substances) Act 1990, when brought into force, will enable local authorities to decide if the presence of a significant quantity of a hazardous substance is appropriate, taking into account existing and prospective development in the vicinity. The controls will be concerned with the storage and use of substances which could present major fire, explosion or toxic hazards to people in the surrounding area. Hazardous substances consent will be required where a hazardous substance is to be present at or above a specified amount, known as the 'controlled quantity'.

53.   Although local planning authorities have been able to exercise some control over the siting of hazardous substances by imposing conditions on planning permission, hazardous substances may be introduced on to land without development being involved. The new provisions will thus enable control to be exercised in circumstances other than where development requiring planning permission is proposed.

Noise

54.   Noise can affect health and have a direct impact on local amenity. Its impact can therefore be a material planning consideration. It may, for example, be a factor in proposals to use or develop land near an existing source of noise, or where a proposed new development is likely to generate noise. Local planning authorities should therefore make a careful assessment of likely noise levels before determining planning applications. Advice on planning and noise is contained in DOE Circular 10/73 (WO 16/73). Updated advice on this issue, to replace and expand that given in Circular 10/73, will be given in a forthcoming PPG. Advice on the control of noise from mineral workings will be provided in a forthcoming MPG Note.

Access

55.   The development of land and buildings provides the opportunity to secure a more accessible environment for everyone, including wheelchair users and other people with disabilities, elderly people, and people with toddlers or infants in pushchairs. Developers and local authorities are encouraged to consider the issue of access at an early stage in the design process. Local planning authorities should ensure that they are fully informed about ways in which access needs can be met, and can offer appropriate advice to developers. The appropriate design of spaces between and around buildings and of parking provision is particularly important in ensuring good access to buildings. When a new building is proposed, or an existing building is being extended or altered, developers should consider the needs of disabled people who might use the building as a place of work, or as visitors or customers.

56.   Where it is not clear from a planning application that provision for disabled people is being considered, it will always be preferable to resolve the problem through negotiation. Where the public are to have access to the building, the local planning authority should consider the extent to which the securing of provision for disabled people can be justified on planning grounds. The sphere of planning control is limited in this con-

text. Conditions attached to planning permissions which have no relevance to planning matters, will be *ultra vires*. More detailed advice on access issues will be contained in a future Circular.

Cancellation of advice

57.   The following advice is hereby cancelled:

PPG1 (January 1988)

Paragraphs 1-4 and 18-21 of DOE Circular 22/80 (WO 40/80)

ANNEX A: DESIGN CONSIDERATIONS

A1. The appearance of proposed development and its relationship to its surroundings are material considerations, and those who determine planning applications and appeals should have regard to them in reaching their decisions.

A2. Good design should be the aim of all involved in the development process, but it is primarily the responsibility of designers and their clients. Applicants and planning authorities should recognise the benefits of engaging skilled advisers and encouraging high design standards. In considering a development proposal, authorities should recognise the design skills and advice of architects and consider carefully the advice of their own professionally qualified advisers, although the final decision remains that of the authority itself.

A3. Planning authorities should reject obviously poor designs which are out of scale or character with their surroundings. But aesthetic judgments are to some extent subjective and authorities should not impose their taste on applicants for planning permission simply because they believe it to be superior. Authorities should not seek to control the detailed design of buildings unless the sensitive character of the setting for the development justifies it.

A4. Applicants for planning permission should demonstrate wherever appropriate that they have considered the wider setting of buildings. New developments should respect but not necessarily mimic the character of their surroundings. Particular weight should be given to the impact of development on existing buildings and the landscape in environmentally sensitive areas such as National Parks, Areas of Outstanding Natural Beauty and Conservation Areas, where the scale of new development and the use of appropriate building materials will often be particularly important.

A5. The appearance and treatment of the spaces between and around buildings is also of great importance. Where these form part of an application site, the landscape design – whether hard or soft – will often be of comparable importance to the design of the buildings and should likewise be the subject of consideration, attention and expert advice. The aim should be for any development to result in a 'benefit' in environmental and landscape terms.

A6. Development plans and guidance for particular areas or sites should provide applicants with clear indications of planning authorities' design expectations. Such advice should avoid excessive prescription and detail and should concentrate on broad matters of scale, density, height, massing, layout, landscape and access. It should focus on encouraging good design rather than stifling experiment, originality or initiative. Indeed the design qualities of an exceptional scheme and its special contribution to the landscape or townscape may justify departing from local authorities' design guidance.

A7. Planning authorities should encourage applicants to consult them before formulating development proposals. Authorities' consideration of proposals will be assisted if applicants provide appropriate illustrative material, according to the circumstances, to show their proposals in context. It may sometimes be helpful for the applicant to submit a short written statement setting out the design principles of the proposal.

Printed in the United Kingdom for HMSO.
Dd.294634, 3/92, C70, 3385/4, 5673, 186916.

HMSO publications are available from:

HMSO Publications Centre
(Mail, fax and telephone orders only)
PO Box 276, London, SW8 5DT
Telephone orders 071-873 9090
General enquiries 071-873 0011
(queuing system in operation for both numbers)
Fax orders 071-873 8200

HMSO Bookshops
49 High Holborn, London, WC1V 6HB   071-873 0011 (counter service only)
258 Broad Street, Birmingham, B1 2HE   021-643 3740
Southey House, 33 Wine Street, Bristol, BS1 2BQ   (0272) 264306
9-21 Princess Street, Manchester, M60 8AS   061-834 7201
80 Chichester Street, Belfast, BT1 4JY   (0232) 238451
71 Lothian Road, Edinburgh, EH3 9AZ   031-228 4181

HMSO's Accredited Agents
(see Yellow Pages)

and through good booksellers

£2.75 net

Recycled Paper

ISBN 0-11-752630-

9 780117 526303